Mastering Google Maps

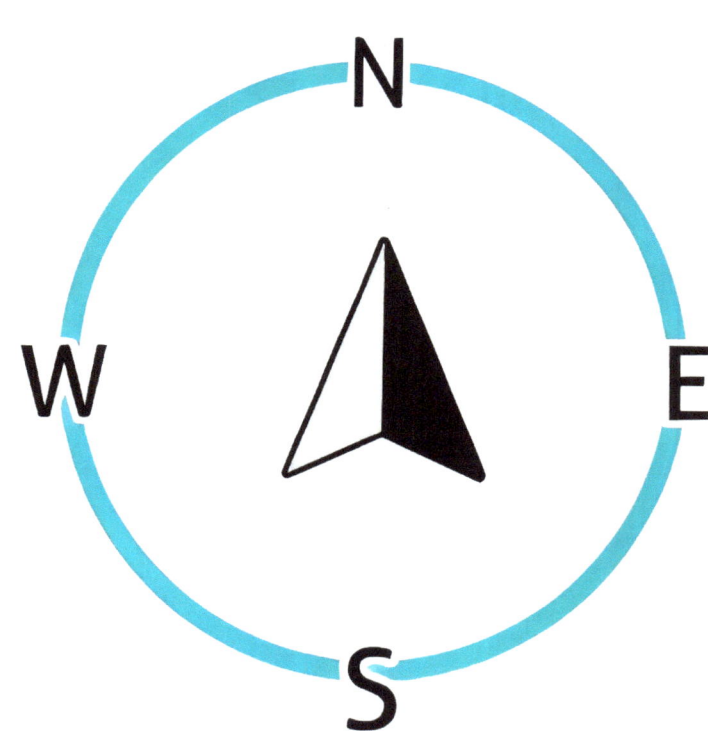

Mastering Google Maps

A Step-by-Step Guide to Navigation and Features

for Seniors

 **PanagiotisAlley**

Copyright © 2024 PanagiotisAlley
All rights reserved.
ISBN: 9798305066487

Table of Contents

page:

Introduction 1
- Overview of Google Maps
- How This Guide Helps Seniors Navigate Easily

Chapter:

1: Getting Started with Google Maps 2

   1.1 What is Google Maps?

   1.2 Downloading and Installing Google Maps

   1.3 Open ing and Setting Up Google Maps for the First Time

2: Understanding the Google Maps Interface. 4

   2.1 Main Features and Tools

   2.2 Using the Search Bar

   2.3 Zooming, Moving the Map, and Switching Views

3: How to Get Directions Using Google Maps. 6

   3.1 Getting Step-by-Step Directions

   3.2 Understanding Turn-by-Turn Navigation

   3.3 Using Voice-Guided Navigation for Hands-Free Directions

4: Exploring More Features. 9

   4.1 Real-Time Traffic and Alternative Routes

   4.2 Saving Favorite Locations (Home, Work, etc.)

   4.3 Finding and Exploring Nearby Places

   4.4 Using Google Maps for Public Transportation

5: Advanced Features for Better Navigation 13

    5.1 Downloading Offline Maps for Internet-Free Navigation

    5.2 Using Google Maps with Voice Commands

    5.3 Sharing Your Location with Family or Friends

6: Troubleshooting and Tips 16

    6.1 What to Do If Google Maps Won't Load

    6.2 Tips for Using Google Maps Effectively

    6.3 Avoiding Tolls, Highways, or Unpaved Roads

Conclusion 17

This table of contents provides a clear roadmap for seniors learning how to use Google Maps, making the guide easy to follow and comprehensive.

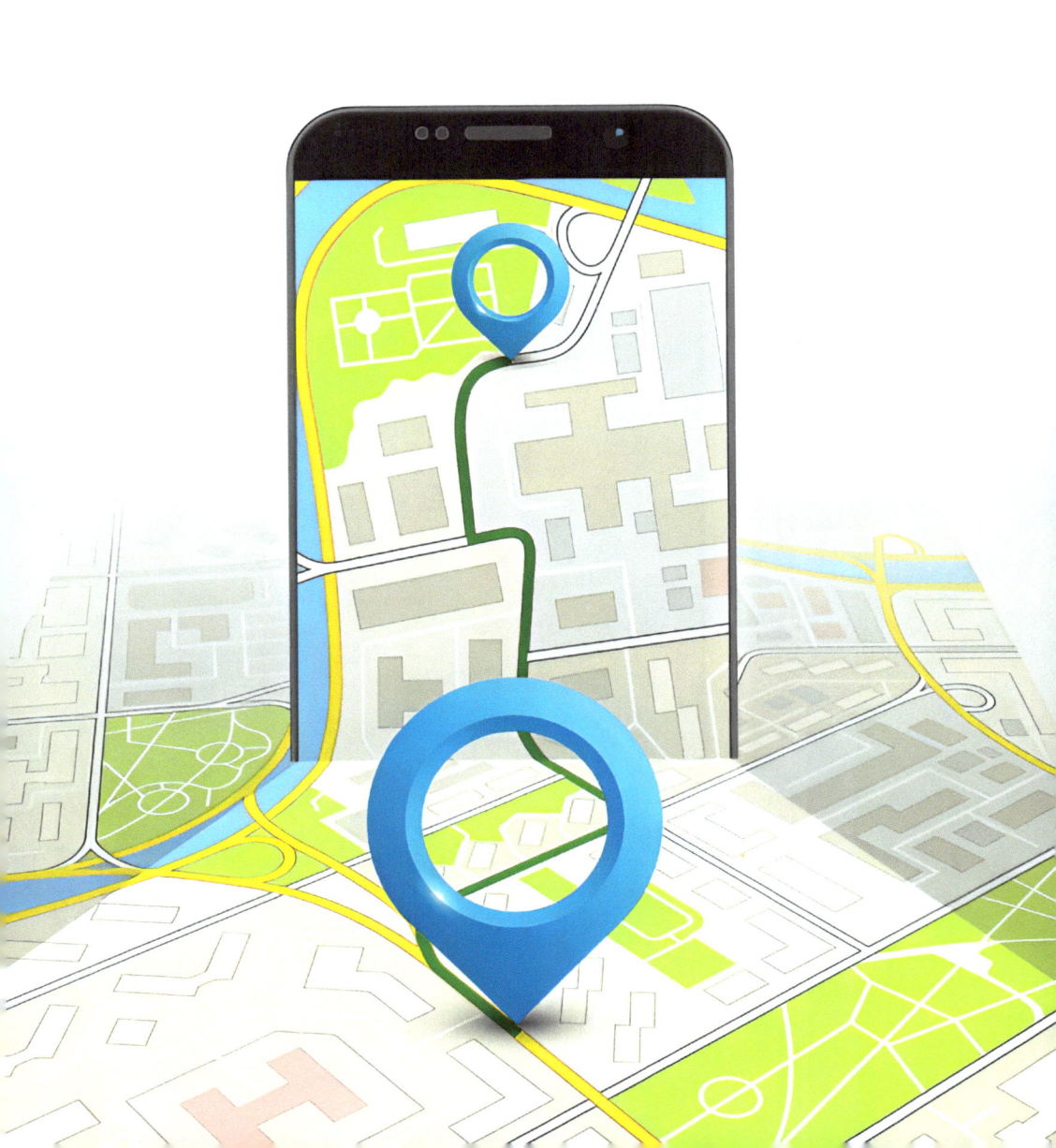

Let's begin your journey into mastering

Google Maps!

Introduction

Welcome to **Mastering Google Maps for Seniors**, your comprehensive guide to learning how to navigate and explore all the features of Google Maps. Whether you're planning a road trip, visiting a new place, or finding nearby attractions, this guide is written specifically for seniors to make using Google Maps an easy and enjoyable experience.

We'll start with the basics and work our way up to advanced features, including how to get step-by-step directions, view real-time traffic, save locations, and even use offline maps when you don't have internet.

Chapter 1

1. Getting Started with Google Maps

1.1 What is Google Maps?

Google Maps is a free app and online tool that helps you navigate, find directions, explore places, and view maps. It's useful for driving, walking, and public transportation. With Google Maps, you can:

- Get directions from point A to point B.
- View real-time traffic updates.
- Find businesses, restaurants, and landmarks.
- Explore places and plan trips.

1.2 Downloading and Installing Google Maps

Before you begin, you need to install the Google Maps app on your smartphone or tablet. Here's how to get it:

1. **Open the App Store (for iPhone/iPad users)** or **Google Play Store (for Android users)**.
2. **Search for "Google Maps"** in the search bar at the top.
3. **O**nce you find the app, tap **"Install"** (or "Get" on iPhone).
4. **W**ait for the app to download and install on your device.
5. **Open** the app by tapping its icon on your home screen.

Chapter 1

1.3 Opening and Setting Up Google Maps

Once installed, it's time to open the app for the first time and set it up:

1. **Tap the Google Maps icon** to open it.
2. **Allow Location Access**: You'll be asked if you want to allow Google Maps to use your phone's location. Tap **"Allow"** so it can find your location.
3. **Sign in (Optional)**: If you have a Google account, you can sign in to save places and access your history. If you don't want to sign in, that's okay—you can still use the app without it.

Now you're ready to start exploring the world with Google Maps!

Chapter 2

2. Understanding the Google Maps Interface

2.1 Main Features and Tools

When you open Google Maps, the main screen may seem busy, but don't worry—everything has a purpose. Let's walk through the key features:

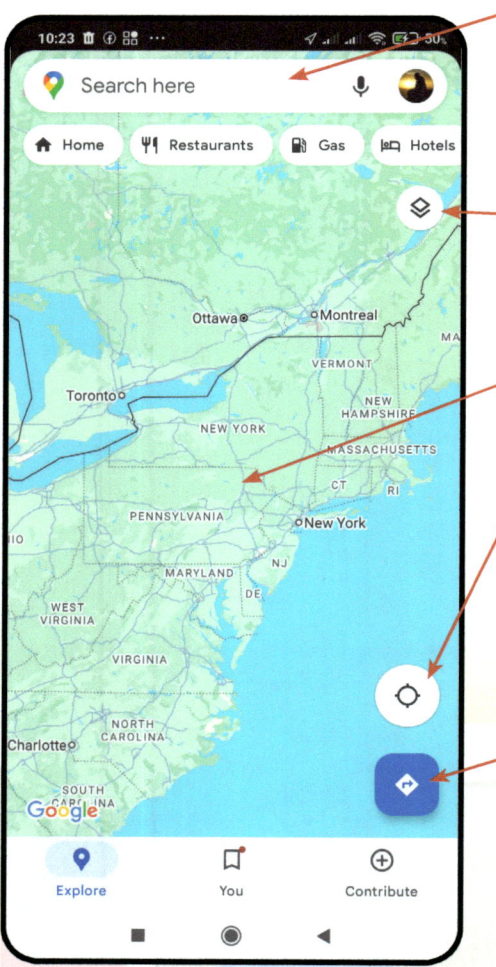

- **Search Bar**: This is at the top of the screen. You'll type the name of the place or address you're looking for here.

- **Layers Button**: This lets you switch between different map views, like satellite or terrain.

- **Map View**: This is the main part of the screen, showing a map of your area.

- **Current Location Button**: A small, round button in the bottom-right corner. It looks like a target. Tap it to find your current location on the map.

- **Directions Button**: It looks like a blue arrow. This will help you plan routes.

5

Chapter 2

2.2 Using the Search Bar

Google Maps allows you to **search for specific addresses**, locations, or businesses easily. Here's how:

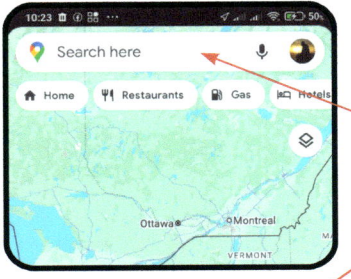

1. **Tap the Search Bar** at the top of the screen.

2. **Type the name** of the place or address you want to go to (e.g., "Grocery store" or "123 Main St").

3. **A list** of possible places will appear. **Tap the correct result**.

4. **You'll now see the location** on the map with details like address, hours of operation, photos and reviews.

5.

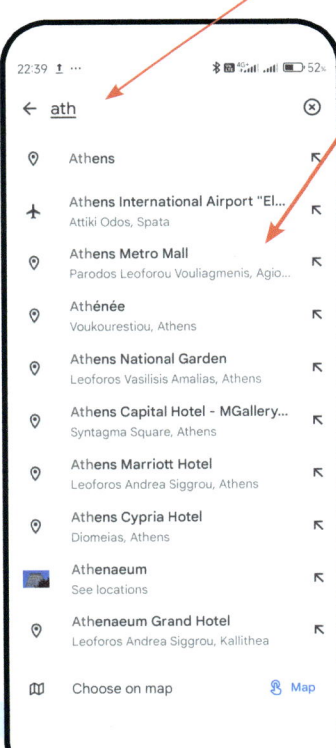

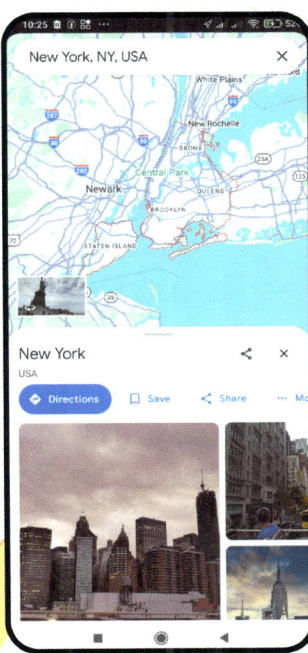

Chapter 3

3. How to Get Directions Using Google Maps

3.1 Getting Step-by-Step Directions

Getting directions is one of the most common uses of Google Maps. You can choose directions for driving, walking, or public transportation.

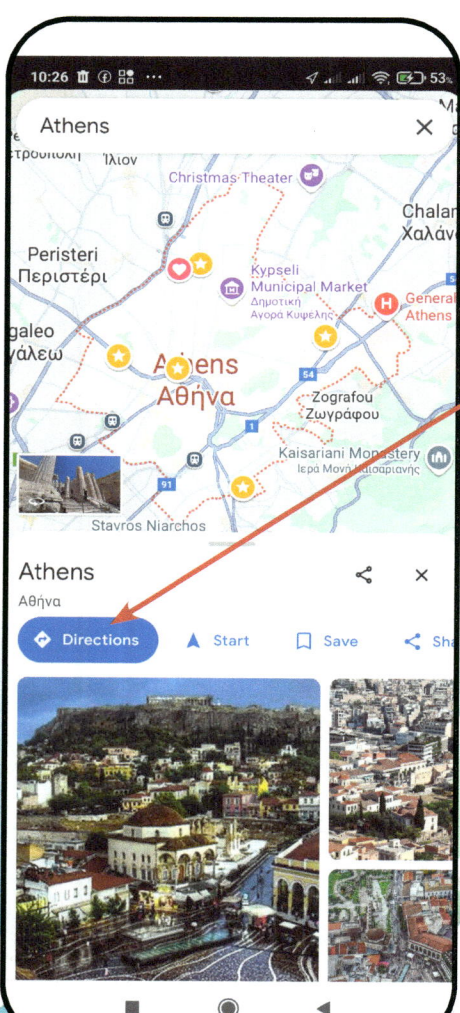

Step-by-Step Instructions:

1. **Search for Your Destination**: Type the location you want to go to in the search bar.

2. **Tap the "Directions" button** under the place's name.

3. **Choose your mode** of transportation:
   - **Car icon** for driving directions.
   - **Bus icon** for public transportation.
   - **Walking person icon** for walking directions.

Chapter 3

4. **Once selected,** you'll see the best route and estimated time of arrival. **Tap "Start"** to begin navigation.

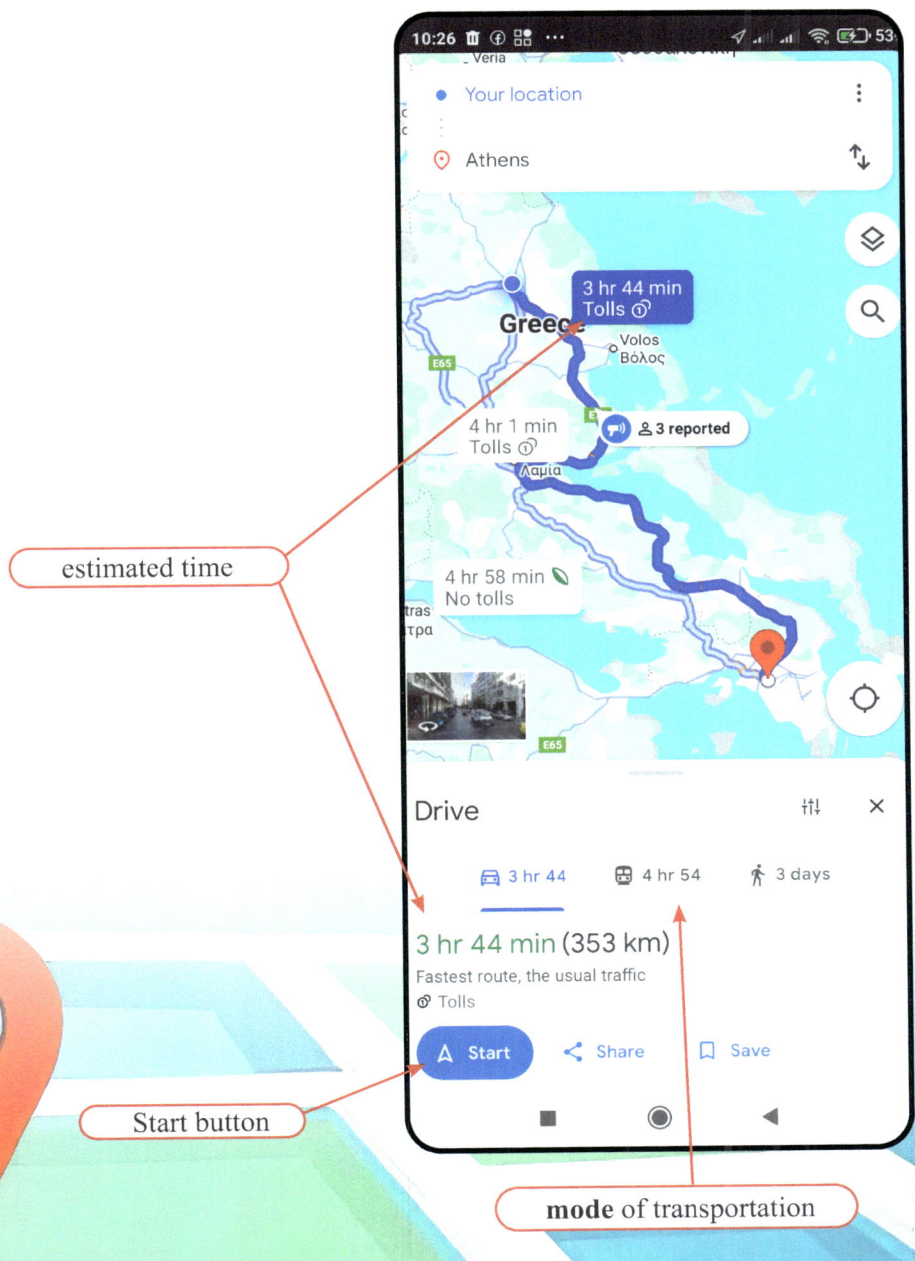

Chapter 3

3.2 Understanding Turn-by-Turn Directions

Once navigation starts, you'll get turn-by-turn instructions, including voice guidance.

1. **Next Turn Indicator**: Google Maps will show you a visual arrow for your next turn.

2. **Distance and Time**: It will also tell you how far the next turn is and how long it will take to arrive at your destination.

3. **Voice Instructions**: You'll hear spoken instructions like, "Turn left in 200 feet." You can adjust the volume of these voice instructions in your phone's settings.

If you make **a wrong turn**, don't worry—Google Maps will automatically reroute you.

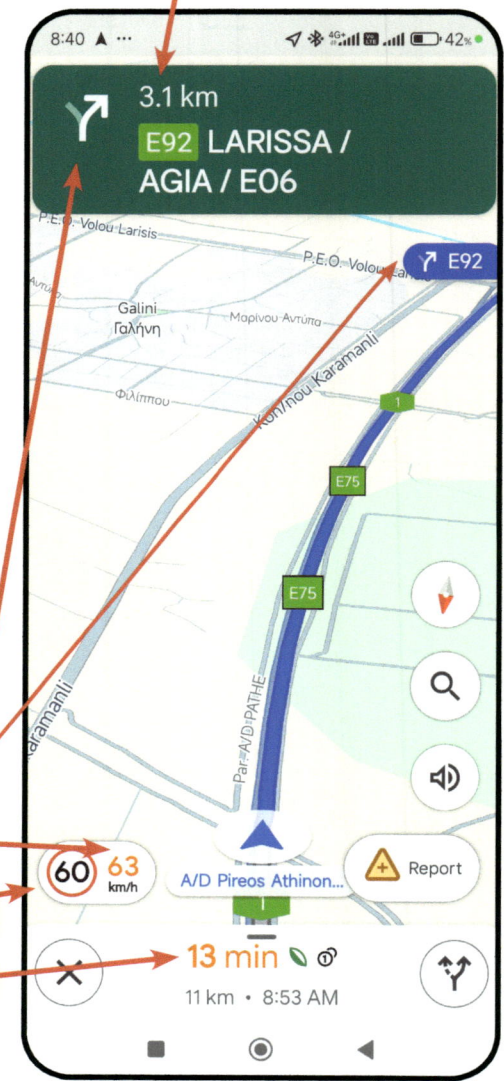

Chapter 4

4. Exploring More Features

4.1 Real-Time Traffic and Alternative Routes

Google Maps offers real-time traffic updates to help you avoid traffic jams.

Step-by-Step Instructions:

1. **Search for a Destination** and tap **"Directions"**.

2. Look at the **color of the roads** on the map:

   - **Green** or **Blue** means no traffic.

   - **Yellow** or **Red** indicates slow or heavy traffic.

3. If there's traffic, Google Maps may suggest **alternative routes** at the top. **Tap on one to switch routes.**

Total route time

Extra time in that route

Alternative routes

10

Chapter 4

4.2 Saving Favorite Locations

You can save your home, work, and favorite spots to access them quickly.

1. Search for **a Place** (e.g., your home address).
2. Tap the **"Save" button** under the place's name.
3. Choose a list like **"Favorites"** or **"Home"**.
4. You can now find this place easily by opening your saved places in the app.

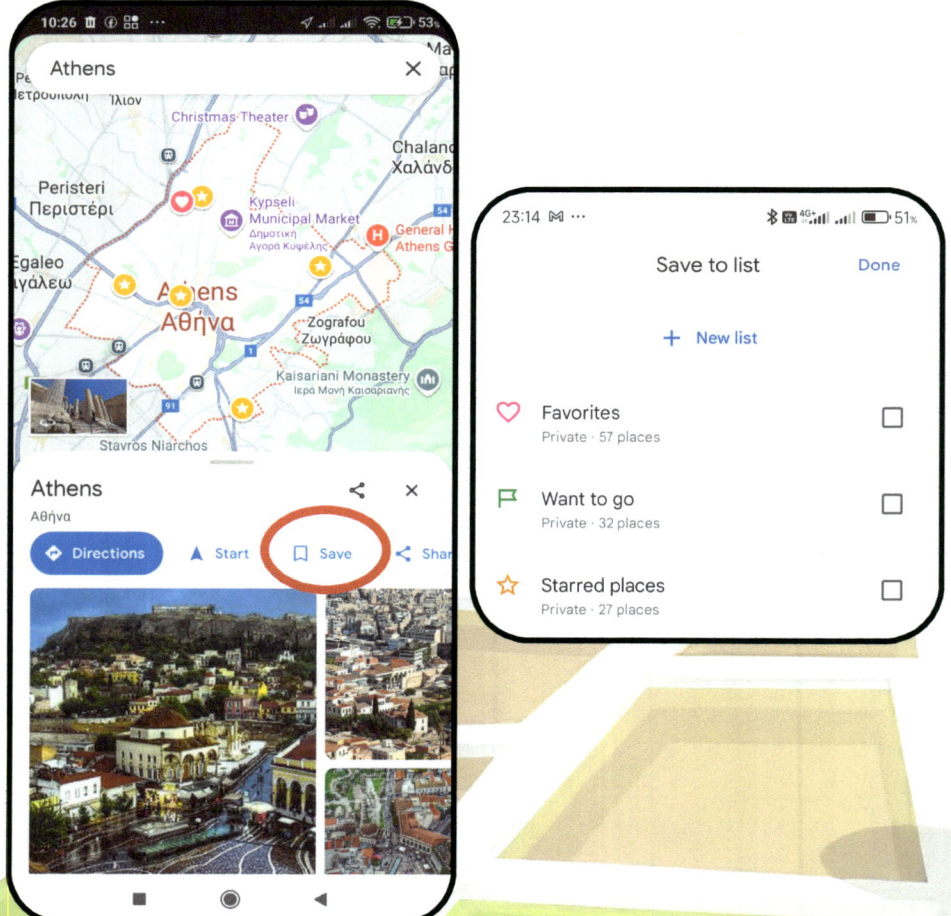

Chapter 4

4.3 Exploring Nearby Places

Google Maps can help you find nearby attractions, restaurants, shops, and more.

1. **Tap the Explore button** at the bottom of the screen.

2. **Select** a category, like **"Restaurants"** or **"Parks"**.

3. **You'll see a list of options** near your current location, along with their ratings and reviews.

- or **Tap an icon** under the search bar and all that places will appear in the map.

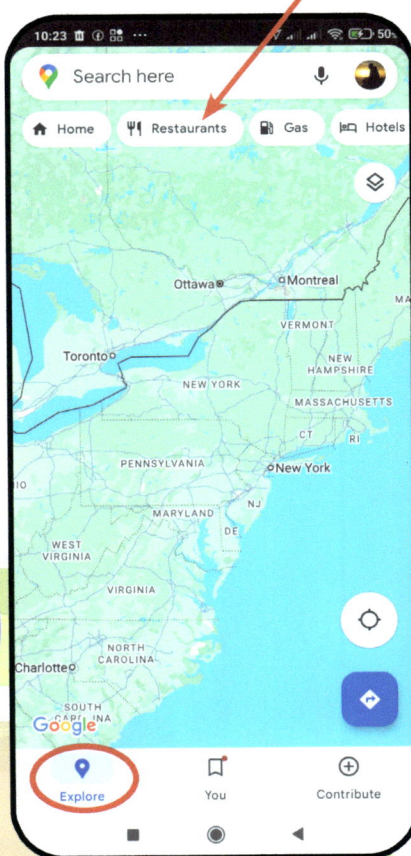 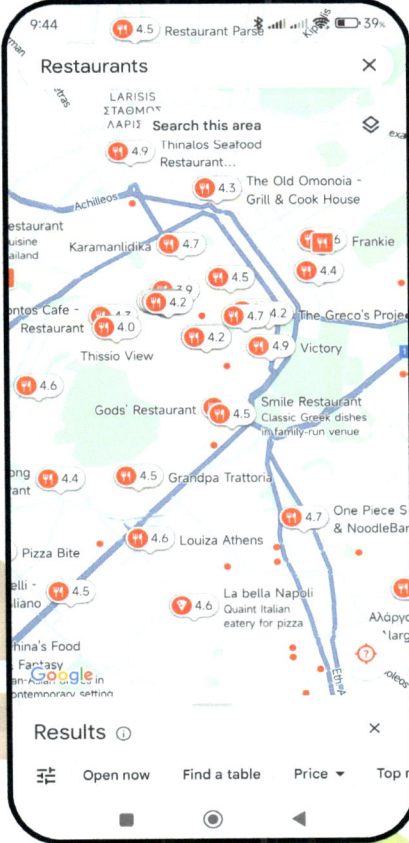

12

4.4 Using Google Maps for Public Transportation

If you prefer public transportation, Google Maps can show you bus, subway, or train routes.

Enter your destination in the search bar.

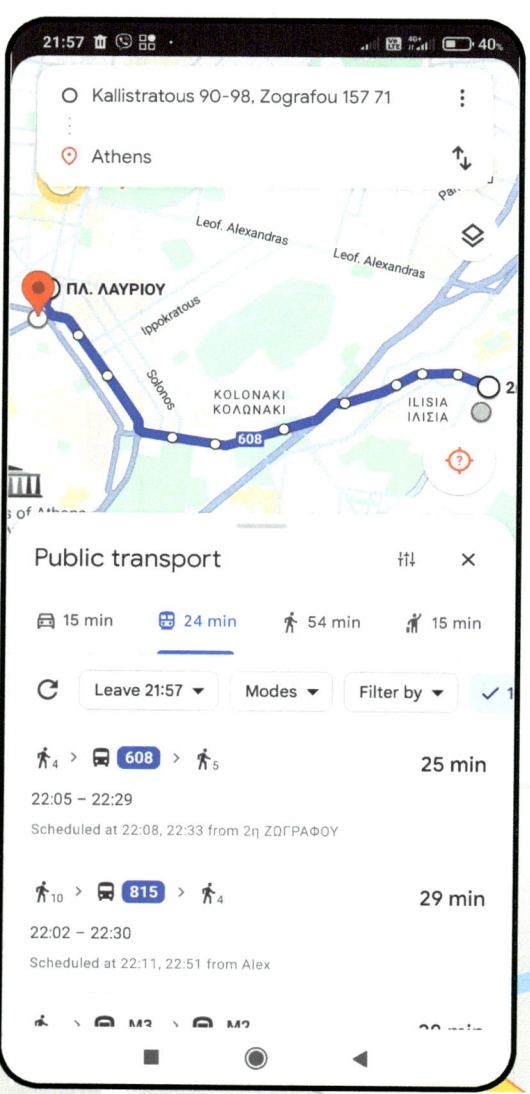

1. Tap **"Directions"** and select the **bus icon**.

2. **You'll see available public transit routes,** including times for the next buses or trains.

3. **Select** the route that works best, and tap **"Start"** to get guidance.

Chapter 5

5. Advanced Features for Better Navigation

5.1 Downloading Offline Maps

If you know you'll be somewhere without internet, you can download maps to use offline.

Step-by-Step Instructions:

1. **Tap on your profile picture** in the top-right corner of Google Maps.

2. **Select "Offline Maps"** from the menu.

3. **Tap "Select Your Own Map"**, and adjust the area you want to save.

4. **Tap "Download"**. You'll be able to navigate that area without an internet connection.

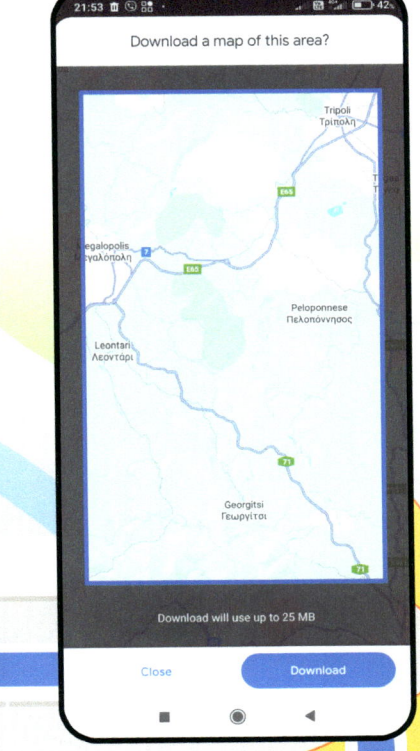
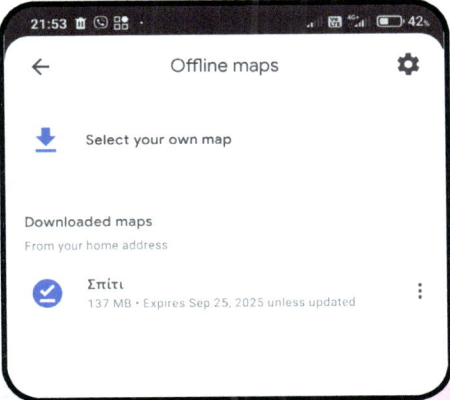

Chapter 5

5.2 Using Google Maps with Voice Commands

To make using Google Maps hands-free, you can use voice commands.

1. Make sure your phone's voice assistant (Google Assistant for Android, Siri for iPhone) is turned on.

2. While driving, say something like, **"Hey Google, navigate to the nearest gas station"**.

3. Google Maps will automatically start guiding you to the nearest station.

4. if you don't want to use phone's voice assistant (Siri or Google Assistant) just click on the microphone icon on the right side of the search bar and say the address you are interested in.

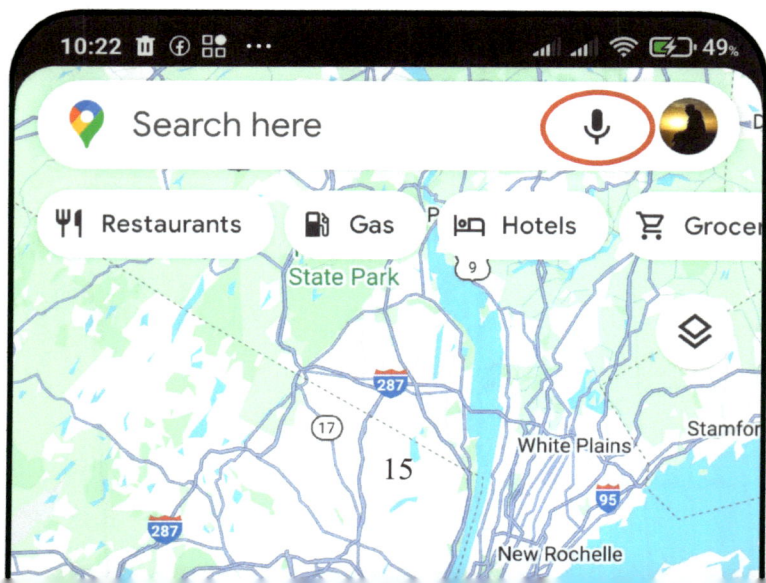

Chapter 5

5.3 Sharing Your Location

You can share your location with family and friends so they can see where you are in real time.

1. Tap your **profile picture** in the top-right corner.

2. Select **"Location Sharing"** from the menu.

3. Choose who you want to share your location with and for how long.

4. Your family or friends will now be able to see your location live.

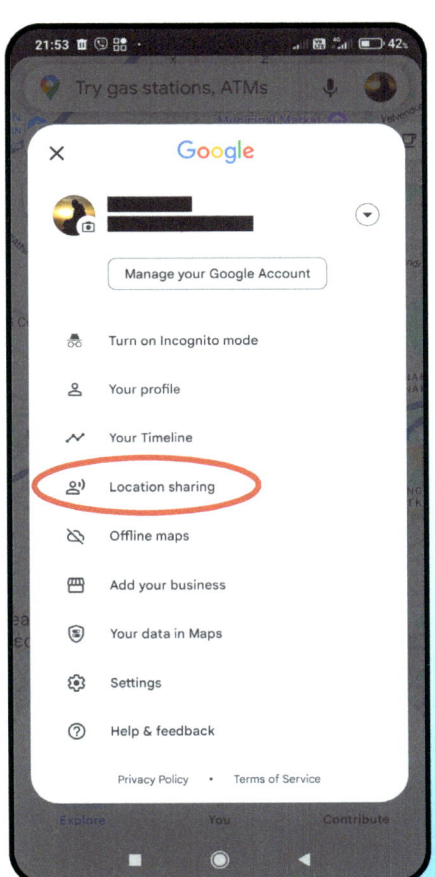

Chapter 6

6. Troubleshooting and Tips

6.1 What to Do if Google Maps Won't Load

If Google Maps isn't working correctly, try these solutions:

- **Check your internet connection**: Make sure you're connected to Wi-Fi or have mobile data turned on.

- **Update the app**: Go to the app store and check for updates to Google Maps.

- **Restart your device**: Sometimes a simple restart can fix glitches.

6.2 Tips for Using Google Maps Effectively

- **Zoom in and out**: Pinch the screen with two fingers to zoom in or spread your fingers to zoom out.

- **Move the map**: Drag your finger across the screen to move the map in any direction.

- **Avoid tolls or highways**: When planning a route, tap "Route Options" to avoid toll roads or highways

Conclusion

Congratulations! You've taken the first steps toward mastering Google Maps navigation. Whether you're exploring a new city or just trying to find the quickest route to the grocery store, Google Maps is a fantastic tool to help you navigate the world with ease. Don't hesitate to explore its features and practice using it—you'll soon become an expert.

Safe travels!

This guide is meant to be a helpful companion on your journey to becoming a confident Google Maps user. By following the steps and practicing, you'll soon find it's an indispensable part of your daily routine. Happy navigating!

We'd Love Your Feedback!

Thank you for taking the time to read Mastering Google Maps for Seniors! We hope this guide has made navigating with Google Maps easier and more enjoyable for you. Your feedback is incredibly valuable to us—it helps improve future editions and ensures we cover topics that matter most to you. If you found this book helpful (or if there are areas where we can improve), we'd love to hear your thoughts! Please consider leaving a review or sharing your experience. Your insights can also help other seniors feel confident using Google Maps. Thank you for being part of this journey, and happy navigating!

Disclaimer

This book was generated with the assistance of artificial intelligence (AI). While every effort has been made to ensure accuracy and reliability, the information provided is based on the capabilities of the AI as of the time of writing and should be used as a guide rather than an absolute source. The creator do not guarantee the completeness, reliability, or accuracy of the information contained within. Any action you take upon the information in this book is strictly at your own risk, and the creator will not be liable for any losses and damages in connection with the use of our guide.

Google Maps!